Inspired

30 DAYS OF INSIGHT & INSPIRATION

SAVINA HIGGS

Inspired 30 Days of Insight & Inspiration

Copyright © 2019 Savina Higgs. All rights reserved.

No part of this publication may be reproduced, stored in a retrieval system, or transmitted in any way, by any means whether electronically, mechanically, via photocopy, recording, or otherwise without the prior written permission of the publisher except as provided by USA copyright law.

Publishing assistance by TJS Publishing House
www.tjspublishinghouse.com
IG: @ tjspublishinghouse
FB: @ tjspublishinghouse

Cover design: Hawkins B Solutions
IG: @ hawkinsb.designs

Published in the United States of America
Savina Higgs Ministries
ISBN-13: 978-0-578-61188-4
ISBN-10: 0-578-61188-0

DEDICATION

I dedicate this book to my mother, Gloria Welch.
Thank you for teaching me the importance of prayer.
I can remember as a child when you would go in the
room and cry out to God on behalf of our family.
Thank you for passing that mantle down to me. I am
the woman I have become because of you.

ACKNOWLEDGMENTS

I cannot express enough gratitude to my tribe for their continued support and encouragement. I offer my sincere appreciation to you all.

The completion of this book could not have been accomplished without the support of my dear sister Sherrie Hoagland and my life coach and friend, Barry V. Hawkins, Jr. Thank you for allowing me to share my vision with you both. I appreciate all your words of wisdom. Thanks for the countless times you would read my quotes and provide feedback.

Finally, to my caring, loving, and supportive husband, Tyrone Higgs, Jr., my deepest gratitude. Your encouragement when the times got rough is much appreciated and duly noted. It was a great comfort and relief to know that you were in my corner.

My heartfelt thanks.

TABLE OF CONTENTS

Acknowledgments	i
DAY 1	1
DAY 2	5
DAY 3	9
DAY 4	13
DAY 5	17
DAY 6	21
DAY 7	25
DAY 8	29
DAY 9	33
DAY 10	37
DAY 11	41
DAY 12	45
DAY 13	49
DAY 14	53
DAY 15	57
DAY 16	61
DAY 17	65

DAY 18	69
DAY 19	73
DAY 20	77
DAY 21	81
DAY 22	85
DAY 23	89
DAY 24	93
DAY 25	97
DAY 26	101
DAY 27	105
DAY 28	109
DAY 29	113
DAY 30	117

DAY 1

I don't worry. God has equipped me for the task.

Jeremiah 29:11 NIV

For I know the plans I have for you," declares the LORD, "plans to prosper you and not to harm you, plans to give you hope and a future."

Repeat this prayer:

Father God, in the name of Jesus, I come to you today asking that you would remove all fear and doubt from my heart. I put my complete trust in you, knowing that you will not put more on me than I can bear. I thank you, God, that I am your workmanship created to do good works. No longer will I allow worrying to keep me from walking into my destiny. In Jesus' name, I pray, amen.

Prayer Notes

DAY 2

God has my back.

Exodus 14:14
NIV

The Lord will fight for you; you need only to be still.

Repeat this prayer:

Father God, in the name of Jesus, thank you for fighting on my behalf. Thank you for giving me victory over the enemy. I no longer try to function in my own strength. I put my complete trust in you. In Jesus' name, I pray, amen.

Prayer Notes

DAY 3

My past and my future have nothing in common.

2 Corinthians 5:17 CEB

So then, if anyone is in Christ, that person is part of the new creation. The old things have gone away, and look, new things have arrived!

Repeat this prayer:

Father God, in the name of Jesus, thank you for making me a new person. I am grateful that you forgave my past. I embrace my new mindset concerning my future. I forever proclaim your goodness. In Jesus' name, I pray, amen.

Prayer Notes

DAY 4

The favor of God shall establish me.

Psalm 90:17 ESV

Let the favor of the Lord our God be upon us, and establish the work of our hands upon us; yes, establish the work of our hands.

Repeat this prayer:

Father God, in the name of Jesus, thank you for seeing my heart. It is a blessing to be chosen by you. I ask that your favor forever be upon my life and that you establish the work of my hands. In Jesus' name, I pray, amen.

Prayer Notes

DAY 5

I will be authentic. What the world needs now is my truth.

Revelation 12:11 ESV

And they have conquered him by the blood of the Lamb and by the word of their testimony, for they loved not their lives even unto death.

Repeat this prayer:

Father God, in the name of Jesus, thank you for giving me victory over the enemy. Thank you for allowing me to be a mouthpiece for the kingdom of heaven. I forever walk in your truth. In Jesus' name, I pray, amen.

Prayer Notes

DAY 6

I am God's masterpiece.

Ephesians 2:10 NLT

For we are God's masterpiece. He has created us anew in Christ Jesus, so we can do the good things he planned for us long ago.

Repeat this prayer:

Father God, in the name of Jesus, thank you for calling me your masterpiece. I no longer believe the lies of the enemy about me. From this day forward, I shall walk in your newness and boldness. In Jesus' name, I pray, amen.

Prayer Notes

DAY 7

My purpose cannot wait.

Proverbs 19:21 NIV

Many are the plans in a person's heart, but it is the Lord's purpose that prevails.

Repeat this prayer:

Father God, in the name of Jesus, thank you for loving me enough to give me a purpose in you. Today I ask that you remove anything in my life that could hinder my purpose. Allow the Holy Spirit to teach me how to operate in my God-given purpose. In Jesus' name, I pray, amen.

Prayer Notes

DAY 8

I will finish strong. Every setback is a divine setup for something greater.

Philippians 1:6 ESV

And I am sure of this, that he who began a good work in you will bring it to completion at the day of Jesus Christ.

Repeat this prayer:

Father God, in the name of Jesus, I believe that you will finish what you started in me and bring it to full completion. I thank you for preparing me for greater. In Jesus' name, I pray, amen.

Prayer Notes

DAY 9

God is waiting for me to put it all in his hands.

1 Peter 5:7 NLT

Give all your worries and cares to God, for He cares about you.

Repeat this prayer:

Father God, in the name of Jesus, I release all my cares to you. I rejoice in knowing that you are always with me. I no longer allow myself to be burdened down with the cares of life. In Jesus' name, I pray, amen.

Prayer Notes

DAY 10

When I pray, God gets involved.

Philippians 4:6 ESV

Do not be anxious about anything, but in everything by prayer and supplication with thanksgiving let your requests be made known to God.

Repeat this prayer:

Father God, in the name of Jesus, thank you for the power of prayer. I yield my will to yours. I find joy in knowing I can make all my requests known to you. In Jesus' name, I pray, amen.

Prayer Notes

DAY 11

It is time
to unpack all
the baggage
I carry
around.

Romans 8:1
ESV

There is therefore now no condemnation for those who are in Christ Jesus.

Repeat this prayer:

Father God, in the name of Jesus, I thank you that I no longer carry around baggage of hurt, guilt, or shame. I receive my healing, forgiveness, and freedom in you. In Jesus' name, I pray, amen.

Prayer Notes

DAY 12

I have been transformed.

2 Corinthians 5:17 ESV

Therefore if anyone is in Christ, he is a new creature; the old things passed away; behold, new things have come.

Repeat this prayer:

Father God, in the name of Jesus, thank you for transforming me. I am a new creature. My inner and outer man reflect the perfect image of Christ. In Jesus' name, I pray, amen.

Prayer Notes

DAY 13

Faith and doubt cannot occupy the same space.

Hebrews 11:1 NIV

Now faith is confidence in what we hope for and assurance about what we do not see.

Repeat this prayer:

Father God, in the name of Jesus, I no longer allow doubt to hinder my faith. I am not moved by what I see. I have full confidence that all things are working together for me. In Jesus' name, I pray, amen.

Prayer Notes

DAY 14

I have
a heart
of gratitude.

1 Thessalonians 5:18 NIV

Give thanks in all circumstances; for this is the will of God in Christ Jesus for you.

Repeat this prayer:

Father God, in the name of Jesus, my heart is full of gratitude towards you. Songs of thankfulness are forever on my lips. In Jesus' name, I pray, amen.

Prayer Notes

DAY 15

My time is valuable. I must always protect it.

Ecclesiastes 3:1 ESV

For everything, there is a season and a time for every matter under heaven.

Repeat this prayer:

Father God, in the name of Jesus, may I be a good steward over the time you give me. I walk in the time and season of your will. In Jesus' name, I pray, amen.

Prayer Notes

DAY 16

It is time to break up with unforgiveness.

Ephesians 4:32 ESV

Be kind to one another, tenderhearted, forgiving one another, as God in Christ forgave you.

Repeat this prayer:

Father God, in the name of Jesus, thank you for forgiving me of all my sins. Allow me to display the very same forgiveness and love to others. Remove any unforgiveness from my heart. In Jesus' name, I pray, amen.

Prayer Notes

DAY 17

I decree and declare I am a magnet for success.

Luke 1:37
ESV

For nothing will be impossible with God.

Repeat this prayer:

Father God, in the name of Jesus, thank you for giving me success in you. I praise you for making all things possible. Success follows me all the days of my life. In Jesus' name, I pray, amen.

Prayer Notes

DAY 18

I will not complain.

Ephesians 4:29 ESV

"Let no corrupting talk come out of your mouths, but only such as is good for building up, as fits the occasion, that it may give grace to those who hear."

Repeat this prayer:

Father God, in the name of Jesus, thank you for forgiving my complaining. I ask that you remove all corrupt talk from my lips. I only speak on matters that uplift the kingdom of heaven. In Jesus' name, I pray, amen.

Prayer Notes

DAY 19

Distraction is my biggest enemy.

Proverbs 4:25 NLV

"Let your eyes look straight in front of you, and keep looking at what is in front of you."

Repeat this prayer:

Father God, in the name of Jesus, I thank you for the power to stay focused. I will keep my eyes stayed on you. No longer will I allow myself to become distracted. In Jesus' name, I pray, amen.

Prayer Notes

DAY 20

A delayed start will not disqualify me from reaching my destiny.

Philippians 3:14 NIV

I press on toward the goal to win the prize for which God has called me heavenward in Christ Jesus.

Repeat this prayer:

Father God, in the name of Jesus, I declare I shall press towards my destiny in you. Thank you for not allowing my delayed start to disqualify me. I give you praise for still being in the race. In Jesus' name, I pray, amen.

Prayer Notes

DAY 21

I do not focus on proving the naysayers wrong.

1 Peter 3:9 CEV

Don't be hateful and insult people just because they are hateful and insult you. Instead, treat everyone with kindness. You are God's chosen ones, and he will bless you.

Repeat this prayer:

Father God, in the name of Jesus, I thank you for a heart to show kindness and love at all times. Give me the ability to always trust your Word over my life. In Jesus' name, I pray, amen.

Prayer Notes

DAY 22

I serve every negative thought in my mind an eviction notice.

Philippians 4:8 NIV

Finally, brothers and sisters, whatever is true, whatever is noble, whatever is right, whatever is pure, whatever is lovely, whatever is admirable if anything is excellent or praiseworthy think about such things.

Repeat this prayer:

Father God, in the name of Jesus, thank you for a new mindset. I command every negative thought to be removed from my mind. I think thoughts of peace and goodness. In Jesus' name, I pray, amen.

Prayer Notes

DAY 23

My tears are watering my purpose.

Psalm 126:5 NIV

Those who sow with tears will reap with songs of joy.

Repeat this prayer:

Father God, in the name of Jesus, thank you for using my tears to water the seeds of my purpose. I declare I shall reap songs of joy. In Jesus' name, I pray, amen.

Prayer Notes

DAY 24

God is
Not looking for me
to be perfect.

He is looking for me
to accept his perfect
will.

Matthew 6:10 NIV

Your kingdom come, your will be done, on earth as it is in heaven.

Repeat this prayer:

Father God, in the name of Jesus, may your perfect will be manifest in my life. I accept all that you have for me. In Jesus' name, I pray, amen.

Prayer Notes

DAY 25

I rest in God.

Jeremiah 31:25 ESV

"For I will satisfy the weary soul, and every languishing soul I will replenish."

Repeat this prayer:

Father God, in the name of Jesus, I find rest in you today. Thank you for replenishing me in every area of my life. In Jesus' name, I pray, amen.

Prayer Notes

DAY 26

I shall have divine friendship in this season.

Proverbs 27:17 ESV

Iron sharpens iron, and one man sharpens another.

Repeat this prayer:

Father God, in the name of Jesus, thank you for connecting me with the right friends in this season. In Jesus' name, I pray, amen.

Prayer Notes

DAY 27

Maturity in Christ makes me love others, forgive others, and help others.

Ephesians 4:13 NIV

Until we all reach unity in the faith and in the knowledge of the Son of God and become mature, attaining to the whole measure of the fullness of Christ.

Repeat this prayer:

Father God, in the name of Jesus, I am thankful that through you, I am able to love, forgive, and help others. In Jesus' name, I pray, amen.

Prayer Notes

DAY 28

The more I keep trying to do it my way, the longer it will take.

Proverbs 3:5 NIV

Trust in the Lord with all your heart, and lean not on your own understanding.

Repeat this prayer:

Father God, in the name of Jesus, I surrender my plans to you. I no longer lean on my understanding. I put my complete trust in you. In Jesus' name, I pray, amen.

Prayer Notes

DAY 29

Never apologize for growing.

2 Peter 3:18 ESV

But grow in the grace and knowledge of our Lord and Savior Jesus Christ. To him be the glory both now and to the day of eternity. Amen.

Repeat this prayer:

Father God, in the name of Jesus, allow me to continue to grow in you. In Jesus' name, I pray, amen.

Prayer Notes

DAY 30

Procrastination will kill my purpose.

Proverbs 13:4 ESV

The soul of the sluggard craves and gets nothing, while the soul of the diligent is richly supplied.

Repeat this prayer:

Father God, in the name of Jesus, I repent for being sluggish in operating in my kingdom purpose. Thank you for redeeming the time on my behalf. In Jesus' name, I pray, amen.

Prayer Notes

ABOUT THE AUTHOR

Savina Higgs is the visionary leader of Savina Higgs Ministries, a platform used to inspire people to pray and lead a life of purpose. Embracing her North Carolinian roots, Savina enjoys doing life with her husband, Tyrone. Learn more by connecting with Savina on social media @justsavina.

www.ingramcontent.com/pod-product-compliance
Lightning Source LLC
Chambersburg PA
CBHW020912090426
42736CB00008B/599

9780578611884